Persuasive Presentations

Steven M. Bragg

AccountingTools®

ISBN 978-1-64221-278-5

Table of Contents

About the Author

Steven Bragg, CPA, has been the chief financial officer or controller of four companies, as well as a consulting manager at Ernst & Young. He received a master's degree in finance from Bentley College, an MBA from Babson College, and a Bachelor's degree in Economics from the University of Maine. He has been a two-time president of the Colorado Mountain Club, and is an avid alpine skier, mountain biker, and certified master diver. Mr. Bragg resides in Centennial, Colorado. He has written more than 300 books and courses, including *New Controller Guidebook*, *GAAP Guidebook*, and *Payroll Management*.

Steven maintains the accountingtools.com web site, which contains continuing professional education courses, the Accounting Best Practices podcast, and thousands of articles on accounting subjects.

Buy Additional AccountingTools Courses

AccountingTools offers more than 1,500 hours of CPE courses, with concentrations in accounting, auditing, finance, taxation, and ethics. Related courses that you might like include:

- Better Business Writing
- How to Run a Meeting

Go to accountingtools.com/cpe to view these additional courses.

AccountingTools®

Persuasive Presentations

Introduction

Presentation excellence comes from an iterative process of writing, rehearsing, and making adjustments – many times. It is rare indeed when someone can speak from rough notes and still convey a powerful message. Instead, a presentation of just a few minutes might require hours of thought. Why devote so much time to the task? Because presentations are designed to persuade the audience. That is, they are a force multiplier – a great presentation convinces others to act, which can result in a much more definitive outcome than if the presentation had convinced no one. In this book, we discuss the key elements of a persuasive presentation.

Persuasion

Persuasion is the process of changing a person's attitude or behavior toward something, using the written or spoken language to convey a combination of feelings, reasoning, and information. Doing so in a presentation is an art form, requiring substantial amounts of preparation work and insights into the thought processes and motivations of attendees. The outcome should be a voluntary choice by the audience to accept the presenter's message, usually because the presenter has correctly chosen a message that clarifies what the audience stands to gain by accepting his or her primary message. What they can gain usually involves one of the following:

- *Money*. The presenter focuses on how the audience can make more money, such as by adhering to her presentation on how to flip homes in record time and at a large profit. The message needs to be ultra-clear, such as, "if you install our new direct-drive motors, your electricity expense will drop by $35,000 per year."
- *Fear*. The presenter can play to the fears of the audience, dwelling upon how much the audience can lose if they ignore her recommendations. For example, "imagine what might happen if you don't install our closed-circuit television system – someone could steal everything in your house!"
- *Efficiency*. The presenter targets solutions that will save time for the audience or generally make their lives easier. For example, "our artificial intelligence system will collect your overdue receivables for you – which might save you 20 hours a week, and avoid that annoying hassle of calling deadbeats."
- *Outcomes*. The presenter shows how the audience can achieve specific desired outcomes. For example, "if you use our services, we can get the government of Abkhazia to approve your building permits within 30 days, so you can have a production facility up and running within six months."

- *Risk*. The presenter shows the audience how to reduce their risk. For example, "if you use our flood mitigation program, we can keep your research facility high and dry."
- *Prestige*. The presenter can show how the audience can achieve a higher degree of fame and/or prestige, such as "we can get you in the door with Sony Music, and you'll be a country music star this time next year!"

The targeted use of one of the preceding items makes it much easier to construct a truly persuasive presentation.

Next, we work through the eight steps of developing a persuasive presentation, most of which occur well before the presenter walks in front of the audience.

Presentation Step 1: Know the Audience

In order to develop an effective presentation, you first need to understand the audience. When a presentation is precisely tailored to match the needs and interests of the audience, when it encompasses their perspective, it is most likely to succeed.

Understanding the audience is not so easy, because it is likely going to be a mix of people with different interests, and who are in attendance for different reasons. For example, one person may be a senior manager, and so is there to pick up information about the strategic aspects of your presentation, while another person is from the sales department, and so is more interested in how to sell your product to customers, while a third person is from the field support team, and so is interested in repairability and warranty issues. These examples focus on the positions of attendees. Other differentiating factors may include a person's age, education, values, and personality.

It is impossible to craft a presentation that appeals equally to everyone on the audience. Instead, understand which audience members will have the greatest impact on the adoption of the idea being presented. For example, for the sale of a software installation, the most important person in the audience might be the IT manager, while for the sale of a forklift, it might be the warehouse forklift driver. While there may be other people in the audience, these specific individuals are the target audience.

EXAMPLE

You are about to meet with the management team of a prospective client, Underwater Anomalies, to pitch them on the idea of using a new form of side scan sonar that can reveal images on the ocean floor spanning an area a mile wide. This greatly reduces the amount of search time needed to find sunken ships and airplanes – which is their specialty. Having a strong knowledge of the characteristics of the client's management team allows you to tailor the presentation to their unique characteristics.

The exploration director, Dirk Ponto, is interested in efficient searches, so the presentation needs to cover the reduction in search time for each unit of one square mile. The engineering manager, Rudi Towson, is most interested in maintenance intervals and product downtime. Finally, Loren Markowitz, the imaging manager, wants to know about the centimeters of resolution provided by the sonar at various depths. Since all three of these managers must agree on the purchase, you will need to devise a presentation that provides each of them with the information they need.

In the preceding example, we guesstimated the needs of the audience based their job titles. To gain a greater understanding of their individual needs, consider the following additional questions about them:

- *Who are they?* The very first step is learning about who they are – at the most basic level, this means their names, titles, and responsibilities. You can delve much more deeply to learn about their educations, work experience, race, sex, political leanings, and – critically – whether they are decision makers. And beyond even this level of detail, learn about who they are as people. Are they sports fans? What hobbies do they have? Do they have children? With this level of detail in hand, it is much easier to formulate a presentation that takes their personal characteristics and needs into account.
- *How many will there be?* Find out how many people will be attending. This figure drives several aspects of the presentation, such as the size of the room, the number of handouts, and the need for audio projection equipment. A larger audience requires more energy and attention-grabbing activities, which can be toned down for a smaller audience.
- *What is their personality type?* When the audience is a small one, consider their personality types, and tailor the presentation to that. For example, a senior executive is more likely to be a strong decision maker, in which case he or she is more concerned with a short, to-the-point presentation. Conversely, someone with a more detail-oriented mindset, such as an IT or accounting person, might want to discuss matters in more detail, including the pluses and minuses of each option presented. If the audience is a happy-go-lucky crowd, then play to that mindset. Conversely, a presentation to an introverted actuary might require a different approach.
- *What is their greatest concern?* What causes the attendees to lose sleep at night or what causes them the most frustration? This is a major point, since if you can address it, you can convert the audience to your side, no matter what else you say during the presentation. For example, if the company you are presenting to has just been hacked and lost a few million credit card records, this would logically be the central point of discussion if you are trying to sell encryption software to them.
- *How do they operate?* What is the company culture? Perhaps they have a strong focus on employee retention, or maybe it is a dog-eat-dog environment, or maybe senior management is constantly pushing the staff to develop new products before the holiday season begins. This can be useful for devising the tone of the presentation, to make it appear that you understand how they view the universe.
- *Why are they here?* Did they come for a specific purpose, or were they told to attend? For example, during a road show presentation, the attendees may

all be stockbrokers who are attending for the free lunch, and who have to be back in the office in less than an hour. If they want just one thing (other than lunch), such as information about a stock pick to convey to their clients, then be sure to give it to them. Otherwise, the meeting will be a waste for everyone.

- *How can you help?* Is there something specific that you can do to improve their situations? If the attendee at a meeting for rocket testing equipment is mostly interested in preventing sealant failures, you can specify how your product can detect potentially catastrophic engine failures, thereby keeping her from being fired. How you can help needs to be stated clearly during the presentation – don't rely on the audience to figure it out for themselves.

- *What do they already know?* If the audience already has significant expertise in the subject matter, then you can strip out basic information and go straight to your primary message. Also, if they are already familiar with the basic industry jargon, you can include it to save time, or exclude it when that is not the case. This approach sets two thresholds; not to be perceived as talking down to them, and not to be perceived as talking over their heads.

- *What is their attitude?* The nature of the presentation may be entirely different, depending on whether the audience is pleased or disgruntled going into the meeting. For example, when there have just been layoffs, the mood of the audience will be entirely different from the situation if bonuses have just been paid out. Thus, the presentation needs to be structured to deal with the expected attitudes of the attendees.

- *What is the call to action?* Based on the previous points, what is the specific thing that you want the audience to do? Buy your product? Volunteer to help your nonprofit? Go forth and reduce carbon emissions? Stating the call to action clearly focuses your attention on what needs to be included in the presentation.

- *What is the main point for the audience to remember?* What single thought do you most want the audience to remember after the presentation has been completed? Whatever it is, be sure to weave it into numerous spots in the presentation, including bullet points, graphics, and data, to ensure that it takes hold.

- *How might they resist?* Are there any reasons why they might not come around to your point of view? If so, address each point of resistance in the presentation, with workarounds. For example, if you expect that a chain of convenience stores will not be able to afford your multi-million-dollar proposal to build adjacent car washes, then also offer them a leasing option in order to spread out the cost. Or, if the installation of automation in a factory is going to result in fewer jobs, make note of the company's job retraining program.

It can be quite difficult to learn about the preceding items, which raises the risk that you will enter a presentation "cold," without enough information about the audience to empathize with them. There are several ways around this problem, including the following:

- *Advance discussions*. One of the best options is to talk to some of the expected attendees a few days in advance, to ask them what they want to get out of the presentation. In particular, talk to the managers who will be in the audience, since they are more likely to be the decision makers.
- *LinkedIn*. Look up their profiles on linkedin.com, or some similar site that aggregates information about people.
- *Office visit*. Visit the company's headquarters or branch office, especially if it offers tours of the facilities.
- *Industry analyses*. Investment analysts may have created industry analyses for the company's industry. These analyses can be quite detailed, including a variety of competitive factors and the relative positioning of the various competitors.
- *Internet search*. Conduct an Internet search on key attendees. There can be a surprising amount posted online for some people.
- *Social media*. Look up their posts on social media, which can provide great clues about what is important to them.
- *Press releases*. Look up the company's press releases, which may be conveniently aggregated on the investor relations page of its website. Other related sources are company newsletters and marketing materials.
- *Web site*. Review the company's website for related information. A good target is the "About Us" page.
- *Annual reports*. Look up the company's annual reports, which may also be listed on the investor relations page on its website.

From the preceding research, extract anything that you might have in common with the audience, in order to find areas of relatability that can be expressed in the presentation. For example, you may have worked in the same industry, have experienced similar events, have similar goals or values, or a similar education. Any of these commonalities can be used to develop the core message of a presentation. For example, you have been asked to make a presentation to fellow employees about a downturn on the company's market, which is the oil and gas industry. You could point out that you have personally been through five layoffs in the industry, due to sharp declines in the price of gas, to which many people in the audience can probably relate. You can proceed from there to talk about the use of hedging to stabilize prices, which will minimize the need for layoffs in the future. Given the group's shared interest in not losing their jobs, it is quite likely that the audience will be *extremely* interested in your presentation.

The in-depth nature of the preceding analysis topics might seem to be overblown. However, if your presentation is critical (*the* make-or-break sales call for your company), then it makes sense to spend the maximum possible amount of time learning every last scrap of information about the audience. Arguably, it would be a dereliction of duty to do anything else.

Summary

Knowing the audience is the cornerstone upon which a presentation is built. Unfortunately, it is also an area to which many presenters give little time, resulting in poorly-targeted presentations. Instead, block out significant time at the start of the presentation preparation process to collect information about the audience.

Presentation Step 2: Develop the Message

Developing and expanding upon the message is an essential part of persuading the audience to follow your recommendations. In this section, we cover the concepts of changing audience behavior, presenting a call to action, and dealing with any residual audience resistance, along with several related issues.

Changing Behavior

When developing the presentation, the essential task is to change the behavior or beliefs of the audience. This means identifying where the audience is now, where you want them to be, and how to span the difference. The information gathered in the first step, about knowing the audience, is crucial to how the message is developed. For example, you will be meeting shortly with an angel investor, who is skeptical about the efficacy of your new carbon capture device, since you will be asking her to invest $500,000 of her own money into rolling out the device. Your goal is to get her so excited about the innovative nature of the device and its potential to generate sales that she will hand you a $500,000 check at the end of the meeting. In many cases, this transformation is a difficult one for the audience, especially when their current position is based on years of first-hand experience – so put yourself in their shoes and ask yourself what it would take to convince you, if you were in the audience.

Getting the audience to move from their position to your position requires you to state the main point of the presentation, which requires use of an action verb to gain their attention. For example, to get a government to switch away from an electronic vote-taking system and toward your paper-based system, the main point could be, "Hackers can alter your vote counts unless you switch to a paper-based voting system." This example presents the danger of remaining with the current scenario, while revealing a solution. By presenting in this manner, you are making the audience uncomfortable with the status quo, while showing them a way to alleviate their pain. In essence, the presentation creates tension, and then uses your solution to resolve the tension. The following exhibit contains several examples.

Presentation Tension and Resolution Statements

Statement to Create Tension	Statement to Resolve Tension
Unfiltered water supplies put your children at risk	Our chemical filtration system eliminates 12 possible water-borne diseases
Understaffing is causing excessive customer wait times	Our outsourcing solutions can cut your customer wait times by 50%
The company has been losing sales for the past three years	We can expand into the northwest region to increase sales
The widget stamper is the key bottleneck in our production process	We can buy a second widget stamper to eliminate the bottleneck

Stating the main point as an action verb seems obvious, but most presenters do not use it. Instead, they simply state the topic, such as "Voting Systems," which is hardly engaging. That approach only looks like you are presenting a status report, instead of a call to action.

The Call to Action

To change an audience's behavior, you must insert a specific call to action into the presentation. This call to action specifies the exact action they should take, and when to do so. Here are several examples:

- If you care about stray puppies, come to our organizational meeting next Tuesday at the elementary school! [asking for participation]
- We need to fund this research on advanced lung cystic fibrosis, and we can do it with a contribution of $1,000 from each of you. [asking for resources]
- If you want to keep oil drillers out of our backyards, then please – contact your state representative today! [asking for influence]
- We need to counter the methane emissions from paddy rice fields, so please send me your suggestions for replacing rice with other crops that have reduced emissions profiles. [asking for ideas]

Dealing with Resistance

A key consideration in changing the behavior of the audience is to spend time thinking about every logical argument that can be presented *against* your presentation. Become familiar with these arguments, and consider how to counter each one – because they *will* be brought up, either during or after the presentation. This work also gives you a deeper understanding of the topic under discussion, and may bring up flaws in your presentation that need to be fixed.

It is also possible that your presentation will run up against the beliefs of the audience, perhaps in such sensitive areas as religion or politics. Running into a person's belief structure will likely tank a presentation, so the main point is to learn about these issues in advance and then structure the presentation to avoid them.

There may be some elements of a presentation that will seriously conflict with the available resources. For example, the announcement of a software installation will require that the accounting staff work weekends for three consecutive months. When these issues come up, state the workaround within the presentation, such as offering double-time pay during the conversion period and a week of paid time-off as soon as it is over. Otherwise, the audience tends to tune out as soon as they have identified a problem.

When you know that there will be a few hard-core critics in the audience, it can make sense to meet with them in advance to discuss their concerns. They may have a number of valid points, which you can address during the presentation. This is also a good time to make a short presentation to the critics, to address the highlights of what you will be talking about during the main presentation. Doing so may reduce their resistance to some extent.

Presentation Tailoring

An essential element of a presentation is to tailor it to the needs of the audience. The best possible outcome is for them to enthusiastically take action, so focus the presentation on how it can help them. For example, talk to a group of business managers about why a specific course of action will cut their effective tax rate. Or, describe to a group of city planners why a new water management system can cut their water requirements by 20% over the next five years. A presentation will be especially effective when it is designed to get the audience out of a difficult situation. For example, when the audience is a company in a region where the supply of electricity is questionable, design the presentation to show how the use of solar panels and a battery backup system will eliminate their downtime and allow them to service customers in a timely manner. This is a better approach than simply detailing the specifications of the system and what it will cost.

Senior Management Presentations

The message developed for senior management needs to be significantly different from a presentation for almost any other party, since this group's needs are different. They have little time available and need to make significant decisions quickly, so their main focus is on obtaining the required decision-making information – right away. For this group, the best option is to provide them with a concise summary of your main points right away, including findings, conclusions, and recommendations within the first few minutes. If the audience wants to keep going after that, then have more slides available that cover additional points of interest – but be prepared to present the key points within just the first few minutes and then shut down the presentation, or let the managers drive the conversation from there.

Tip: When dealing with executives, state up front that you will cover the key points of the presentation within the first few minutes. Doing so may keep them from interrupting for that period of time.

Development Best Practices

It can be difficult to assemble discussion points for a presentation. Fortunately, there are a number of best practices available that can make the work easier. Consider the following options:

1. *Look for similar presentations*. Other people may have made presentations about similar subjects. If so, see if they are available, either in-house, through a trade association, or over the Internet. Perusing them can give you clues about how your presentation should be structured.

2. *Brainstorm*. Write down ideas on post-it notes and slap them on a white board. This will initially be a messy conglomeration of ideas. Then reshuffle the post-it notes into a more coherent form and organize them into a logical flow that can be used in a presentation. This works best with several people, since they can generate more ideas.

3. *Pare it down*. The first version of a presentation is almost always too long. Review it multiple times, and extract anything remotely superfluous. The intent is to end up with a tightly-focused message where the primary idea is presented, and everything else supports that idea. Or, stated differently, data overload is one of the best ways to destroy a presentation.

EXAMPLE

A company is looking for additional funding to support an expansion of its land database products. The first pass at the presentation covers all three divisions of the company and the expertise of the various company managers. However, the main focus of the presentation is supposed to be getting funding for database development, so several iterations later, all mention of the other divisions and the managers has been stripped out. The final version simply states the nature of the products to be developed, the expected sales from each one, and the funding needed to create them.

Tip: When there is a lot of information that could go into a presentation, retain just the key points for the presentation, and assemble everything else into a handout that can be distributed after the presentation has been completed. Do not hand it out in advance, since everyone will be leafing through it, which distracts them from the presentation.

4. *Organize*. Write down the title of each slide, and see if the flow of the presentation makes sense. Change the order if necessary. Also, avoid passive title wording; for example, replace "Market Share" with "We are Losing Market Share!" Once the ordering of the titles makes sense, add bullet points beneath each one.

5. *Lay out the structure*. The presentation should have a beginning, a middle, and an end. The contents of each phase should cover the following topics:

a. *The beginning.* The beginning should be very quick, spanning no more than one or two minutes. In it, the goals are to welcome the audience, tell them who you are, and state the purpose of the presentation. For example:

> Good morning everyone, and thanks for coming! My name is James T. Kilpatrick, and I have most recently been the controller of the starship *Enterprise*. The purpose of today's presentation is to show you how the new Vulcan Accounting Meld (VAM) software can automate most transactions and allow for mental control of the system. We'll start with the problems you're having right now with your current system, and then I'll show you how the Vulcan system can solve them.
>
> My presentation should take about 20 minutes, which will leave plenty of time for questions and answers at the end. Of course, please feel free to ask a question at any time!

b. *The middle.* The middle section is comprised of your key points, supporting comments that expand upon those key points, and a statement regarding how to get from the audience's current situation to the more ideal future state. Try to keep the number of key points down to three, which makes them easier to remember (see the following tip about the forgetting curve). Since there are so few points, make them count. The best key points will be of particular interest to the audience and are closely tied to the call to action that appears at the end of the presentation. For example:

1. The VAM software can track dilithium crystal usage, so the ship does not run out of fuel. I understand that this happened to you during the last run to the Epsilon Indi system.
2. The VAM software can track turnover among the red shirted personnel, so that replacements can be scheduled at the next port of call.
3. The VAM software can aggregate expenditures for multiple ship departments, including the bridge, transporter room, sick bay, engineering, and security.

It can be useful to insert transition statements between these key points. By doing so, you are signaling that the preceding point has been completed, and that you are moving along to the next one. These statements keep the audience engaged with the flow of the presentation. For example:

> [transitioning between Points 1 and 2 in the preceding discussion]
>
> Since we've just talked about dilithium crystal usage, let's also talk about personnel usage – specifically the red shirts who keep dying off. Let's move to Point 2 and see how the VAM software can keep track of these unfortunate events...

Supporting comments are designed to bolster the key points. They may involve the recitation of facts, an attempt to generate emotions among the audience, or (better yet) a combination of the two. Examples of supporting comments are customer testimonials, personal stories, quotations, photos, cost analyses, market research, and so forth. The comments chosen should fit within the time constraints of the presentation and impact the decision-making of the audience. For example:

> The VAM software has already been installed on the USS Drake, USS Ajax, and USS Dakota. In all three cases, the starships reported being able to extend their tours of duty by an average of six weeks through proper monitoring of their dilithium crystal usage.

Tip: The *forgetting curve* hypothesizes the decline of memory retention over a period of time, where 50% of the information presented is lost within one hour, and 90% within one week. Based on these results, it makes sense to focus the attention of the audience on quite a small number of key points (such as three), since a larger quantity will not be retained.

---

c. *The close.* The closing section includes a summarization of the key points made in the middle of the presentation, followed by a call to action, and a statement of thanks for attending, perhaps pointing out the person who arranged the meeting. Begin this section with the statement "In summary," to signal the approaching end of the presentation; they tend to sit up and listen harder at this point. Then move immediately into what the key points were and how they benefit the audience. And finally, state the call to action – the one essential item that you want the audience to take away from the presentation. For example:

In summary, the Vulcan Accounting Meld software can help you avoid being dead in space, restock your red shirt personnel, and ensure that no ship departments are running over on their expenditures. In short, this is the ideal starship management tool. I encourage you to purchase the VAM software if you want to drastically improve the performance of your ship. I am leaving a proposal with you to review; it outlines the all-in cost of the software, as well as our proposed implementation timeline.

Thank you for coming, and my thanks to Commander Riker, who arranged this meeting.

Or, stated more succinctly by Andrew Carnegie, use the beginning to tell the audience what you are about to tell them, use the middle to do so, and use the ending to tell them what you just told them.

EXAMPLE

The point to be made is that the company needs a coordinated way to identify and disposition obsolete inventory.

The beginning statement is that the company wrote off $100,000 of obsolete inventory in the past year. [states the current situation]

The middle of the presentation notes that there is no organized system for evaluating the status of inventory [the current situation]. However, if a materials review board were to be assembled, consisting of representatives of the materials management, accounting, and engineering departments, we could identify these items with quarterly meetings. Though this will require time, we estimate that doing so will allow for early disposition of any inventory tagged as being potentially obsolete, which could save the company $60,000 per year. [compares current to future situation]

The ending statement notes that the loss can be reduced to just $40,000 per year, as long as the three departments can spare one person each, four times a year. This will also result in better purchasing and disposal procedures, which may further reduce the loss within the next few years. [states the benefits, and describes the exact commitment needed]

This beginning/middle/end format is an easy way to structure a presentation, and so should serve as the baseline payout for most presentations.

6. *Add emotional weight*. It is too easy to simply make a facts-based presentation, which does not grip the audience. Instead, find a few spots in the presentation where an emotional connection can be inserted. For example, rather than merely laying out a number of cost cutting measures in a presentation, an emotional hook would be "and if we don't cut costs by at least 10%, the

company will fold and everyone will lose their jobs." Ideally, an emotional hook should be strong enough to inspire the audience to change.

7. *Add startling numbers.* If there are any truly unusually factoids that will grab the attention of the audience, work them into the presentation. For example, "the opioid epidemic in Harrison County resulted in more deaths last year than the county suffered from battle deaths in all of World War II."

8. *Screen out jargon.* If there is any jargon in the presentation that the audience might not understand, eliminate it or at least explain what it means. Otherwise, there is a strong risk of losing the audience.

9. *Be quotable.* The best presentations always contain a few great sound bites that the audience will remember – perhaps long after they've forgotten the rest of the presentation. The best quote is one that conveys the essence of the presentation. For example, when presenting to an audience of distributors about why you are revamping the entire product line, the words "because quality comes first," repeated throughout the presentation, will stamp in their minds exactly why the change is being made.

10. *Include stories.* Depending on the situation, it can make sense to include a story to which the audience can relate, and which supports the main point of the presentation. For example, a presentation about a new exercise regimen could include a story about how it has transformed someone's life.

Ideally, the presentation should be quite short. A 15-minute presentation is better than a 30-minute presentation, and in some cases an even shorter presentation will have the most impact. When planning the amount of content to include, block out 40% of your allotted time for audience questions – which, of course, shortens the duration of the presentation even more.

Summary

The presenter usually has a massive pile of information from which to craft a presentation. The trick is to assemble a streamlined message, using only as much text as necessary, to persuade the audience. Too much information, and the audience will be confused. Too little information, and they will not be persuaded. Arriving at just the right balance is the main goal of Step 2, developing the message.

Presentation Step 3: Identify the Media

There tends to be an automatic assumption that a presentation will be accompanied by slides, which were probably developed using PowerPoint. However, the proper media to be used really depends on the audience. For example, a very small group of a few people might prefer a handout, while a larger group might find a video to be more entertaining. Generally, the audience size and level of spontaneity drives the type of media used. The various options are:

- *Small audience, casual setting.* Tends to be a short presentation with supplementary white board or presentation board supplementary material.

- *Small audience, interactive.* Tends to include printed materials and/or slides, after which a white board, flipchart, or butcher paper may be used to write down audience comments.
- *Large audience, formal setting.* Tends to be a rehearsed presentation with slides and/or videos.
- *Large audience, canned presentation.* Has been recorded in advance in the same manner used for a large audience in a formal setting, possibly with an audio voice-over, for on-demand streaming.

It is usually useful to include some sort of visuals in a presentation, since this triggers a substantial increase in audience retention of the message being conveyed. Besides information retention, here are several additional reasons why visuals are a good idea:

- The visuals control the flow of the presentation, since the audience tends to focus almost exclusively on the points appearing before them.
- The audience shifts its attention away from the presenter, which can give the person a small break while they absorb the information on the slide.

However, be prepared for the negative effects of a technology glitch, such as a loss of power or a projector failing right in the middle of a presentation. If you present enough times, these situations *will* arise, which leaves only one option – the presenter. Keep in mind that the best and most reliable visual aid is always the presenter, so be prepared to forge on without any form of assistance. This can be a real problem for many people, since they tend to use slides as a crutch, and when that crutch is taken away, they collapse. A better approach is to initially practice *without* the aids, and then bring them into a later practice session, once you have mastered the essential points to be conveyed to the audience.

Presentation Step 4: Develop Slides

An audience tolerates ordinary slides, but can be persuaded by great ones. When properly designed to match the message and tweaked to capture the attention of the audience, they can strongly support the speaker's message. Conversely, it would be better not to present poorly-constructed slides at all. In this section, we cover the types of slides that may be used, how they can be improved, and several related topics.

A Few Essential Facts

Before developing slides, it is essential to learn a few key facts about the presentation in which they will be used. Consider the following issues that relate to slides:

- *The time available.* The topic relating to slides is how much time to allot to the presentation. With this information in hand, you can estimate the amount of time per slide, and back into the maximum number of slides that can be presented.

- *Projection equipment.* Will slide projection equipment be available? If not, your choices are to either bring your own projector, or print the slides and issue them as handouts instead.
- *Lighting.* What kind of lighting will be provided in the presentation room? If the lights are too bright, this may make it too difficult for anyone to see the slides, which may call for different presentation arrangements.

Types of Slides

When designing slides, keep in mind that there are a number of different slide formats from which to choose, each of which has its own advantages and disadvantages. The types of slide formats are as follows:

- *Placeholder slide.* This is the slide that is up on the screen when attendees walk into the room. It may display the company logo, or perhaps a title more specific to the presentation.
- *Title slide.* This slide is parked at the beginning of the presentation, and states the title of the presentation, as well as the name, title, and affiliation of the presenter.
- *Agenda slide.* This slide shows the main topics to be covered in the presentation. It can be inserted again later in the presentation, with the next topic highlighted, so that the audience knows where they are in the presentation.
- *Bullet slide.* This slide is used to present a list of related ideas, each one preceded by a bullet. It is the most common slide found in most presentations.
- *Quote slide.* This slide contains a brief quote by someone else, with the appropriate attribution. It is used only occasionally, when a quote dovetails with the concepts being presented.
- *Video slide.* This slide contains a text clip. It can be useful as a break from the surrounding static slides, and can be used to reinforce the point being made. For example, a video slide could show a person being injected with a pharmaceutical firm's new vaccine.
- *Data slide.* This slide contains data relating to the main message, such as a sales trend line, profitability figures by quarter, or unit sales in a new sales territory.
- *Ending slide.* This slide stays up on the screen at the end of the presentation. It may state a call to action, or perhaps the contact information of the presenter.

Slide Improvements

Presentations are either strongly supported or negatively impacted by the quality of the slides being used as visuals. Here are several of the key issues to be aware of:

- *Font size.* Everyone in the group should be able to read the slides. To be sure that the font size is sufficient, do a trial run in the room where the presentation will be held, sit in the back row, and see if you can comfortably read the slides. The sans serif font is easiest to read.

- *Font emphasis*. Use a larger font on the items in a slide that are of the most importance. This may be a substantially larger font if the item of emphasis is relatively short. For example, if the focus is on stating that there was a 92% voter turnout, then the "92%" figure could be in a much larger font than the rest of the statement.

- *Caps*. Use caps for the first letter of the first word on a bullet point item. Never use all caps, since it is the text equivalent of screaming at the audience.

- *Alignments*. Make sure that text blocks and graphics are appropriately aligned. If they are not, this will be quite obvious when the slides are blown up for everyone to see.

- *Color palette*. Minimize the color palette to keep it from being distracting, such as black text and a couple of neutral shades.

- *Contrast*. Maximize the amount of contrast on the slide, to make text easier to read. Therefore, do use black text on a white background, and do not use dark blue text on a lighter-blue background.

- *White space*. This is the open space on a slide that contains nothing at all. It can be quite useful to have a large amount of white space on a slide, since it sharpens the focus of the audience on the few items remaining on it.

- *Illustrations*. If you add illustrations, make them look as though the same person designed all of them. Including a variety of unrelated illustrations makes the entire presentation look unprofessional and thrown together.

- *Number of bullet points*. Minimize the number of bullet points stated on each slide. When the number exceeds four bullet points, shift the additional information to a separate slide. Otherwise, the amount of information being presented will be overwhelming for the audience. Also, limit the number of words for each bullet point to no more than six words.

- *Spelling*. Have someone else proofread the slides to ensure that there are no typos. A misspelling seems to leap off the page at the audience, and significantly reduces their estimation of the presenter's capabilities.

- *Verb structure*. Consistently begin all bullet points with an action verb. Doing so provides consistency, and avoids making passive statements.

- *List presentation*. When showing a list, present just one line at a time. Otherwise, the audience will be busy reading through to the bottom of the list while you are still discussing the top few items.

- *Data presentation*. When presenting data, minimize the amount presented. For example, when the focus is on profitability, only show profits (not any other part of the income statement), and preferably only for a few reporting periods. Otherwise, the audience will find itself wading through reams of data. Other related points are:

    o Color the key data items in bold or rich colors, and everything else in muted tones. Doing so tells the eye where to focus first.

- o Deemphasize labels, axes, and borders. These items only clutter the slide, and the presenter can fill them in if necessary.

- *Transitions*. As long as it is not too distracting, add transition graphics to liven up the move from one slide to the next. This is most useful when you need to break up the tedium of an unusually long presentation.
- *Stylistic consistency*. The slides should look as though the same person created all of them, because they have the same look and feel; this is derived from having a similar layout, font, color palette, and other elements.
- *Slide numbering*. Put the slide number in a corner of each slide. This makes it easier for audience members to make note of a particular slide that they want to return to later, in order to discuss it further.

Tip: To boil down the preceding slide improvement points to a few essentials, use the 10-20-30 rule, which states that a presentation should contain no more than 10 slides, last no more than 20 minutes, and use at least 30-point font.

When taken together, the preceding points should result in slides that an audience can easily assimilate within a few seconds. This is critical, since any time spent looking at a slide will be time *not* spent listening to the presenter. Therefore, each slide needs to be discernible at a glance.

A final though is to adjust slides for the specific audience. In those cases in which the same slide deck is being used for a series of presentations, it can help to make a few references within the slides to the current audience – perhaps their company name, what it does, or the names of a few key people. Doing so makes it easier to form a connection with them.

Slide Problems

It is sometimes better to describe what to *avoid* in slide preparation, rather than extolling which techniques work best. Here, then, are some of the issues that annoy audiences:

- *Pretty slides*. Whenever fancy colors, animation or audio features are added to a slide, they distract from the message. Instead, strip each slide down to its bare essentials, to focus the audience's attention.

Tip: Ditch the attractive company logo that you've inserted into the footer of each slide. They already know who you are, and the graphic distracts from the message.

- *Read-along writing*. Do not put so much text on the slide that it is easier for all concerned to simply read from the slide, rather than making a separate presentation. Instead, the text needs to be as brief as possible.

> **Tip:** If the slides convey the entirely of a presentation, then you've just created a memo, not a presentation. If that is the case, the best option may be to actually convert it entirely into a document and distribute that – rather than scheduling a presentation.

- *Reminders*. Do not structure the slides as a series of reminders for what you want to say. Slides are for the use of the audience, not you. Instead, the slides should only contain whatever it takes to enhance the audience's understanding of the subject matter.
- *Slide count*. Do not include a mass of disparate slides in your presentation and hope to meet your allotted time limit simply by speaking faster. Instead, cut back on the number of slides – possibly by a drastic amount – in order to cut the presentation time and refine the message being delivered. There are many cases in which slides are not needed at all, especially when the presentation involves small groups in a casual speaking environment. It is impossible to recommend an exact number of slides to use, since it varies by so much, depending on the speaker, topic, audience, and so forth. But as a general rule, always look for ways to shrink the number of slides.

EXAMPLE

A speaker has been given a time budget of one hour for an important presentation. She wants to leave half of the presentation open for a question and answer session, which leaves 30 minutes for the actual presentation. A reasonable average for her is to spend two minutes on each slide. That being the case, a good starting point for her is to develop a set of 15 slides to support her presentation.

Slide Alternatives

There are a few alternatives to slides that may be worth considering. Each one has characteristics that may make it more effective than slides, or perhaps as an accompaniment to them. Consider the following options:

- *Presentation boards*. These free-standing display boards can be set up anywhere in the room, and so tend to be used as supplementary displays. However, they are not large enough to convey information within a large room, where a large font size is needed.
- *Flip charts*. These are multi-page pads of tear-away paper on easels. They are useful for jotting down ideas or questions, which can then be ripped off and posted anywhere in the room.
- *White board*. The use of a white board makes sense when the presentation needs to be adjusted on the fly to match the needs of the audience. For example, a salesperson could use a whiteboard to sketch out a networking installation, based on input from the other people in the room.
- *Videos*. A video can be presented, either on a television or onto a screen, to illustrate the points being made. For example, a presentation regarding a new

teaching method could have an accompanying video that shows students using the new method.

- *Butcher paper.* These very large rolls of paper can be cut to any size and taped to the walls, where they are useful for jotting down lengthier process flows and brainstorming ideas.
- *Handouts.* A well-constructed memo that is handed out as an accompaniment can be quite useful as a source of additional information. Alternatively, a printout of the slides that will be presented can be used by attendees to jot down notes about the presentation.
- *Exhibits.* If the presentation involves a discussion of a physical object, such as one of your company's products, bring it out on stage and talk about it. Doing so holds the attention better than a dry recitation of the facts pertaining to that object.

A mix of the preceding options can be quite useful for giving participants a more varied experience, which may pique their interest. For example, during a product presentation, you could vary from a straight speech to a video showing the product being used by customers, to a flip chart on which you write its benefits, to rolling out the actual product and pointing out its features.

Summary

Above all, remember that slides are simply a tool that is there to enhance the speaker's message. Great slides will not result in a great presentation – only the presenter can do that. So, it makes more sense to invest time in preparing your speech than in turning each slide into a polished jewel of graphical display excellence. Instead, use slides to support the presentation, noting key points and graphically illustrating the more abstract ideas that cannot be conveyed so easily through speech.

Presentation Step 5: Practice

The development of the presentation notes and accompanying slides sets the groundwork for a good presentation, but it will go to waste unless you spend a significant amount of time practicing the presentation. In this section, we cover such topics as dry runs, timing, and Q&A preparation.

General Knowledge Level

When practicing a presentation, the goal is not to memorize every line, but rather to have a solid knowledge of what to say. This is a critical difference. If you memorize the presentation word for word, you will come across as wooden, since the entire presentation will be an ongoing struggle to recall precisely what needs to be said. Conversely, if you have a solid knowledge of the source material, all you need to do is glance at the notes to determine what the next topic is, and extemporize from there. In the latter case, this allows you to more easily adapt if the audience asks a question or wants to skip part of the presentation, or the projector fails. The latter approach also makes it less necessary to stay immobilized behind a lectern with your speech. Instead, it is easier to roam around and engage with the audience.

Dry Runs

One of the best ways to practice a presentation is to do so in front of someone who is not invested in the outcome, perhaps a co-worker who is not involved in your project. These people have not been engaged in the work up to this point, and so are in a good position to spot anomalies or logical flaws that you might never have spotted. For example, the practice subject might point out that your presentation stays laser-focused only through slide 6, after which it diverges suddenly in an unexpected direction. Or, they could spot phrases that the audience might consider odd or misleading. This type of analysis is especially useful for spotting slides that do not belong at all, or valid presentation topics for which there is no slide.

After the first few iterations, a dry run should include the accompanying slides or other presentation materials. That way, you can become accustomed to interacting with them as part of the presentation. Doing so can also contribute to the refinement of these materials, since you might tweak them as part of your ongoing adjustments to the presentation. As part of this process, consider examining the following items:

- *Transitions*. See if there are any odd transitions from one slide to the next, and smooth them out.
- *Consistency*. Make sure that the graphic images being used are consistent from one slide to the next.
- *Commentary*. Evaluate whether the commentary that accompanies each bullet point is smooth.

Scale of Discussion Importance

During each dry run, always start with the key takeaway for each slide, so that the audience is absolutely made aware of the main point within a few seconds. Then layer on additional detail in order to expand upon this base layer of information. This second layer can vary in size, depending on the level of audience interest and the amount of time left in the presentation. By taking this two-level approach, you will always be assured of conveying the essentials to the audience. This approach is also appreciated by the audience, which maintains a tight focus on the essential elements of the presentation.

> **Tip:** Do a dry run using just the key takeaways for each slide, and track the amount of elapsed time. Then subtract this from the total time allotted to the presentation, which tells you how much "fluff" time is available for less-critical discussion topics.

Timing

Have someone track the time required to complete each slide in the presentation. Then work back through this information to see if slide topics can be compressed, or perhaps eliminated entirely. When paring back information in this manner, make sure that there is still a logical flow to the presentation; some adjustment of the wording may be required.

Videos

Consider making a video recording of the presentation, perhaps on a smartphone, and assess how you look. Are you making eye contact or looking down at your notes? Do you appear relaxed or wooden? Are your gestures natural or awkward? Whenever there is an issue, work on your presentation and then review it again with another video recording.

Double Endings

It can be useful to plan two endings to the presentation. There can be a normal ending, which assumes that the presentation proceeds at its normal pace. In addition, have another ending ready to use that occurs on an earlier slide. This second ending is needed to wrap things up if any interruptions occur that would otherwise result in an overly long presentation.

Q&A Preparation

There is usually a question and answer section at the end of a presentation. If so, this presents a possible trap for the presenter, since it is no longer possible to rely on a polished presentation. Instead, it is entirely possible that someone will ask a question that calls the point of the entire presentation into doubt, and which may negate all the good effort that has gone into it. Given this risk, it makes a great deal of sense to make a list of every likely (and unlikely) question that someone might ask, and spend time developing replies to each one. Pay particular attention to any hostile questions that may be posed; the audience may be won over if you can handle these with aplomb.

There may be cases in which a question comes for which you simply have no answer at all. When that is the case, say so – don't try to fake a response. Instead, offer to research the question and get back to the group with an answer. Or, if you will be moving on to another city the next day, offer to post the answer on your web site, where they can read it.

If the presentation is to be used multiple times, consider each question and answer session to be an opportunity to collect questions that you have not heard before. Whenever one of these questions arises, put it in your database of questions and come up with a good response to it. Over time, this approach to collecting difficult questions will place you in the enviable position of having a polished answer to every conceivable question.

Understand the Venue

Whenever possible, try to gain an understanding of the venue in which you will be conducting the presentation. How large is the space? Will there be a stage? How will the chairs be arranged? Will there be people attending by videoconference call? What about the projection equipment to be used? Where is the lighting? Are there visual obstructions? Is there a lectern? Will there be a microphone? Will food be served during the presentation? All of these issues can impact where you stand in the room, how your voice will project, and whether there will be problems conveying the information on slides. If the actual venue differs substantially from your expectations, this might throw you off, making for a much more uncomfortable presentation – which will likely be apparent to the audience.

A particular concern is whether your presentation will be recorded for later consumption. If so, remember to look at the cameras frequently, in order to connect with the viewers. In addition, be particularly careful about what you say – no off-color jokes – since the recording is for posterity.

Understand the Order of Presentation

If your presentation will be just one in a string of presentations, make inquiries about the subject matter of the other presentations. You might be able to build into your presentation a reference or two to the topics being addressed by other presenters. Conversely, if you are following someone who will be presenting a contrary viewpoint, consider the impact this will have on the audience – they may not be as amenable to what you have to say.

If your presentation will be towards the end of the day, when people are tired of listening, consider using a shorter presentation, since they will likely tune out towards the end of your talk anyways. Or, if your timeslot will be competing with a more popular event in the next room over, consider what this will do to the size of your audience.

Another issue is whether a moderator will be controlling the flow of the presentations. If so, will she be introducing you, or do you need to prepare a few words about yourself to begin your presentation?

Summary

The preceding discussion should make it clear that a major presentation requires lots of advance work, to the point where you need to start the process one or two months early, leaving enough time to conduct a series of practice sessions, each focusing on different aspects of the presentation.

Presentation Step 6: Deliver the Presentation

The presentation itself is the culmination of a long preparatory process, as discussed earlier in this book. But even at this late date, it is still possible to conduct a less-than-stellar presentation, unless you pay attention to the additional topics noted in this section.

Dress Code

In a presentation, try to match what the audience is wearing. If you dress in a more casual manner, this can be taken as a sign of disrespect, while if you dress more formally than them, it conveys the message that you think you are better than them. So, the trick is to anticipate the audience. This can be accomplished by making inquiries with the organization coordinating the meeting, or by contacting a few people in advance who are expected to be in the audience, and asking them. The dress code is covered more extensively in a later section.

Same-Day Preparation

Delivering the presentation begins an hour in advance, which is ideally when you want to arrive at the meeting room. Such an early start is needed in order to arrange the tables and seating to your satisfaction, and especially to make sure that the technology works. When you are heavily dependent on the accompanying slides, it can feel like a soul-crushing defeat when the projector dies. To minimize this risk, take the following steps:

- Get the contact information for the responsible audio-visual person. Be *very* nice to this person, since you may be entirely dependent on him or her to save your presentation.
- Turn on the projector and microphone and make sure that they both work. Verify that the remote control for the projector is operational.
- If the slides are to be projected from the front, there is a good chance that you will walk into the light beam and obscure the projected image (and also be blinded). To keep this from happening, use tape to mark the projection area on the floor, and stay out of it.
- Have printed versions of the presentation available. This is the backup in case the technology completely fails, so that you can at least give the audience the printed version and walk them through it.
- If you are using audio or video files, make sure in advance that they will run on the laptop that you are planning to use for the presentation.
- Assume the Internet connection will not work, so if you are doing a software demonstration, have the entire demo pre-recorded on your laptop (and backed up again on a thumb drive, in case the laptop fails).
- Run through the entire slide deck, to make sure that no slides have inadvertently been scrambled. A related task is to stand in every possible spot within the presentation area and use the remote control, to see if it has sufficient range to operate the projector. If not, stay away from the dead zones.

Presentation Pointers

The actual presentation can be improved by paying attention to a number of small details, which are noted in the following bullet points:

- *Attitude*. The attitude you have at the start of the presentation sets the tone for the proceedings, so match the attitude to the discussion topic. For example, a chipper attitude would seem reasonable if you are reporting about the company's stellar annual results, while a more somber attitude should be used when discussing a layoff.

- *Stand up*. Always stand up when making a presentation. By doing so, you can more easily be adjacent to the screen, so that the audience can easily see both at the same time. Also, standing allows you to more easily move out into the audience to deal with a question or make a point. And finally, someone who is standing projects more confidence than someone who is sitting down.
- *Position left*. It is customary to stand to the left of the screen, from the perspective of the audience. This works best for a Western audience, which is accustomed to reading from left to right. They begin with the presenter, then read the slide, and then return to the presenter.
- *Set out a watch*. Put your watch or a timer where you can easily see it, and make note of the starting time. This allows you to take note of the passage of time, so that you can expand or contract the material, depending on the impact of audience interruptions. If there is a moderator, he or she can take on this task, noting the amount of time left until you need to finish.
- *Tell them the format*. When beginning the presentation, give the audience an overview – tell them who you are and what the presentation is about, to clarify matters as much as possible.
- *Announce handout distribution*. Tell the audience that a handout containing the presentation will be distributed at the end of the presentation. By doing so, they are forced to listen to you, rather than thumbing through the handout.
- *Be humble*. An overly aggressive or self-focused approach can turn off an audience, so instead take a low-key route. Remember, people buy from people they like, so try to come across as a decent human being.
- *Do not read*. It is inexcusable to read directly from your documents or slides. There is a massive difference between the monotonous drone of someone reading from prepared text and someone who is talking in a conversational tone and making eye contact with the audience.
- *Look them in the eye*. The presenter may glance down at his or her notes occasionally, or look at projected slides briefly, but should mostly be looking straight out at the audience. This is the best way to pull them into the presentation. Conversely, never looking at them alienates the audience.
- *Move around*. A moderate amount of activity gives the impression of being animated about the subject matter. For example, move towards someone when responding to their question, and walk towards the screen when addressing a key point on a slide.
- *Open up*. Try not to cross your arms or clasp your hands. These actions signal discomfort. The audience is more likely to relate to an open, relaxed stance. Also, try to project some emotion (which is tough when you're petrified), since it shows that you care about the subject matter. Also, if the room is a large one, exaggerate your gestures to make them more visible in the back.
- *Avoid the flat delivery*. It is quite common for business people to deliver presentations in a factual tone of voice that rarely varies. While this can make a person sound authoritative, it can also put an audience to sleep, and is

certainly not energizing. Try some variation to break up the flat delivery, such as:

- o Drop in a dramatic pause every now and then. Glory in the silence for a few seconds, and then continue to your next point. A pregnant pause can be quite useful for focusing the attention of the audience on the point that was just made.
- o Tag-team the presentation with a second person, whose speaking style (whatever it is) will certainly vary from your own, and so represents something new and different for the audience.
- o Throw in the occasional question for the audience. Doing so changes the end of the questioning sentence on an upward note, which not only represents a break in your authoritative delivery, but also pulls in the audience – after all, they're supposed to answer the question.
- o Tell a story. Doing so switches you to a conversational style, which will differ from your normal mode of delivery.

- *Avoid furniture.* Standing behind a lectern or desk puts some distance between the presenter and the audience, which adds to the sense of distance in the room. If you are comfortable speaking without these devices, then do so – it improves your connection with the audience.
- *Include the audience.* Encourage the audience to be involved in the presentation. They may want to ask questions, ask for clarification of certain points, or redirect the discussion. When they are deeply involved, they will relate more to the outcome, and so may be more convinced by your call to action at the end. There are several variations on how to do this, which are:
  - o *Ask for questions up front.* This approach can work when you know the material perfectly, and so can adjust your presentation on the fly to accommodate the audience's questions. This option allows for better tailoring of the presentation to the needs of the audience.
  - o *Take questions during the presentation.* When the audience is relatively small, consider encouraging questions throughout the presentation. Doing so can clarify points for the audience on the fly. However, this approach can halt the entire presentation if a difficult question comes up, and a flurry of questions can derail the entire presentation. If there are too many questions, it may be necessary to halt any additional questions until the end of the presentation.
  - o *Take questions at the end.* Taking questions at the end is the most common approach, because there is a clear transition between the presentation and the audience discussion. This approach works well with a large audience, since those with no questions can easily leave the room.

- *Adjust based on what you see.* If you see that the audience is yawning, has their arms crossed, are talking to each other, or are looking at their phones, you may need to adjust the presentation on the fly, perhaps shortening it, or asking if there are any particular points on which they want to focus.

- *Use a laser pointer.* A laser pointer is an excellent tool for pointing out a key item on a slide, and also keeps you from having to walk in front of the projector to point out the specific spot on the screen.
- *Black out the screen.* There may be times when you want the audience to focus solely on you. A good way to do so is to shut the projector off, toggle the screen to black, or insert a blank slide into the presentation. This is most appropriate when you want to tell a story, make a key point, or move out into the audience.
- *Take one question each.* Sometimes, a person in the audience will try to ask a number of questions in a row. This can be disrespectful of other people who might also want to ask a question, especially when the total presentation time is limited. To resolve this problem, state up front that you will answer just one question per person. If someone still tries to ask a string of questions, then just answer the first one, and then move along to another person.

Tip: When possible, use a meeting facilitator. This person fields questions from the audience, recognizes people in the audience, and clarifies their questions. A facilitator also puts a buffer between the audience and the presenter, which can be useful if an awkward question is asked.

- *Monitor social media.* If there is a moderator, have this person monitor social media and send a text message to the presenter's phone if there are any criticisms appearing that should be addressed during the presentation.

Subsequent to the Presentation

If the point of a presentation really is to enact change, then consider taking some follow-up actions that are intended to keep pushing audience members in the direction of your primary message. Here are some possibilities:

- *Host a luncheon.* By sticking around afterwards for drinks or a luncheon, you can make yourself available for anyone who wants to chat further about the presentation.
- *Send a note.* A handwritten note is quite rare these days, which makes its impact all that much greater. This approach works best when the presentation was made to a small number of decision-makers.
- *Send an email.* When the audience is larger, send an email that summarizes the main points of the presentation, and states the next steps that they can follow up on.
- *Call.* When the audience is small and has expressed an interest in following up, call them to discuss how they want to proceed. This approach is usually limited to quite a small number of calls, since it can be time-intensive.

The actions noted here would be most applicable when the initial presentation was only intended to be a foot in the door, as part of a longer process of interacting more fully with people in the audience.

Summary

Ultimately, the outcome of a presentation is founded upon the audience's perception of how it went. If you paid attention to the layout of the room, the lighting, your appearance, the quality of the slides, the coherence of your presentation and enthusiasm for the subject matter, and your rapport with the audience, then this creates a positive perception in the eyes of the audience, which leads to their increased acceptance of your message.

Presentation Step 7: Take Audience Questions

A speaker may do an excellent job of making the initial presentation to an audience, and yet fall apart during the following question and answer session. This more free-form part of the presentation can cause real problems, which can be mitigated by following these points:

- *Anticipate questions*. The best way to deal with audience questions is to write down every possible question that you think someone might ask, and then come up with a plausible answer to each one. By doing so, your responses will appear to be much better-crafted than would normally be the case. Also, consider asking your colleagues for additional questions, to expand the pool of possible questions that may be posed.
- *Rehearse replies*. Assuming that you have derived a set of anticipated questions, your next step is to rehearse answers out loud, and preferably in front of someone who can provide feedback.
- *Preempt questions*. If you know that a question will be asked, bring it up yourself and answer it. Doing so keeps this issue off the table, allowing more room for other questions.
- *Wait*. Do not start answering a question until the person posing the question has finished. There is a natural tendency to cut a person off when you know the answer, but doing so is disrespectful and gives you the appearance of being impatient. In addition, cutting someone off might also mean that you are cutting off a second part of the question. To be sure that you understand a question fully, paraphrase it back to the questioner, ask clarifying questions as necessary, gain the person's affirmation, and then proceed to your answer. Even then, consider waiting an extra moment to gather your thoughts; doing so gives you some extra time in which to compose a reply, and also gives the impression that you are giving the person's question a sufficient amount of consideration.
- *Talk straight back*. When responding to an audience member, talk straight back to that person, perhaps even taking a few steps toward him or her, and

definitely maintaining eye contact. By doing so, you are signaling that 100% of your attention is focused on that person.

- *Be courteous.* There may be times when you are tempted to snipe back at a person who is causing you difficulty. However, treating everyone with courtesy will gain the respect of the audience (though perhaps not that specific questioner), so contain your emotions at all times.
- *Avoid guessing.* If you don't know the answer, then say so right away. Trying to fake an answer is worse, since it undermines your credibility with the audience. Your best approach is to offer to research the question and get back to the questioner later with an answer. An alternative is to ask the rest of the audience if they can provide the answer.
- *Be short.* Answer questions as briefly and succinctly as possible, especially when the question and answer session is short. Doing so allows for more questions to be asked, which gives you more feedback about what might need to be fixed in your presentation the next time around. If a longer answer is required, offer to do so after the presentation is over.
- *Remind them of the big picture.* It is quite likely that someone will nitpick minor points in your presentation. When this happens, remind them that your solution addresses the big picture of what they need, which is not affected by these minor points.
- *Deal with cost.* When your price is higher than that of the competition, point out the extra service level or product features that you are bringing to the table, which the competition cannot do.
- *Use an accepting mindset.* When the audience asks questions, consider each question to be an opportunity to better understand their problems. With this accepting mindset in place, you will be more eager to write down the best objections, so that you can make an even better presentation the next time.
- *Summarize again.* At the end of the question and answer session, take a few moments to reiterate the summarization that you already made earlier. Doing so ties up the presentation neatly, and leaves the audience with your key points, rather than the response to the last question asked.
- *End on time.* Be respectful of the audience's time, which means ending on schedule. This is easier when a moderator is present, since it is that person's job to monitor the remaining time available for questions.

Presentation Step 8: Measure the Presentation Impact

Any presentation can be improved, but this can only be done when the audience provides useful feedback. There are several ways to obtain it, including the following:

- Hand out survey forms at the beginning of the presentation, and ask them to leave a completed form on their chairs before they leave.
- On the final slide of the presentation, state a web page on which they can write comments.

- If anyone sticks around after the presentation, ask them for a realistic appraisal of how the presentation went.
- Email audience members or hand them a survey after the presentation is over, though the response percentage tends to decline significantly once people have left the room.
- View what the audience is saying on social media; though sometimes harsh, there may be nuggets of useful information that can be applied to future versions of the same presentation.

The Importance of Having a Connection

The part of a presentation that the audience remembers the most is typically something that involves them directly, so it is critical for the speaker to form a connection with them, which can then be used to involve them in the presentation, as noted in the following sections.

The Connection with the Audience

An essential element to keep in mind when constructing a presentation is that a key element is not part of the presentation materials – it is your connection with the audience. They will relate far better to someone who is a good storyteller, or who has a good sense of humor, or who inspires them, or who is clearly sincere (and preferably all of them at once!). We did not discuss the development of these attributes in the prior sections, because they cannot really be planned. It is not feasible to put a bullet point in the notes that says, "at this point, be sincere!"

The way to develop a connection with the audience is to stop trying to deliver a perfect, word-for-word presentation, and instead to walk around (wonderful for loosening up), chat with the audience, tell stories that relate to the subject matter, and generally extemporize *around* the subject matter. The result is a much looser and flowing narrative that allows the audience to see who you really are, and why your core message is so important. Conversely, don't try to deliver a word-for-word perfect presentation, because there will be inevitable slip-ups, which will nip away at your confidence and (more importantly) interfere with any incipient connection that you might have been developing with the audience.

The Different Learning Styles

People in the audience may have different learning styles. They may absorb information better if it is presented to them visually (such as through a chart), audibly (through the speaker's voice), or by touch (where they participate in the presentation or examine an object). A great presentation is designed to cover all three learning styles. For example, the presentation of a consumer electronics item will likely involve the presentation of a specifications table (for visual learners), several presenters extolling its virtues (for the auditory crowd) and a hands-on demonstration (for those who need to touch it). This multi-layered approach is more likely to impress the audience as a whole.

Audience Involvement

In addition to the different learning styles, the speaker needs to recognize that the people in the audience likely have considerable experience in the subject matter, and so may be interested in participating in the presentation. That being the case, the presenter can strive toward more audience involvement by pausing occasionally to ask for questions or comments, or to involve them in a brief group discussion. By bringing several people into the discussion, they become more engaged with both the speaker and the subject matter. And, since they are most likely to remember that part of the presentation that involves them, be sure to meld the key points of the presentation into these audience participation segments.

It is essential to make audience involvement an affirming experience for them. Since this is a group setting, no one wants to be belittled in front of their peers, so always be polite and respectful when discussing any issue with an audience member. If there is a point of disagreement, then agree to disagree, rather than getting into a shouting match.

Audience Involvement Techniques

There are many ways in which to involve the audience in a discussion. Consider the following choices:

- *Ask for introductions*. For a smaller group, have each person in the audience introduce themselves. This typically includes their name, job, and anything they want the group to know about them. This is not necessary when they already know each other.
- *Ask for a takeaway list*. Ask the audience what they want to take away from this presentation, making a list on a flip chart to one side. Then work through the list as part of the presentation.
- *Ask for volunteers*. It can be useful to bring someone to the front of the room, either as part of an exercise or to assist in writing down information on flip charts or butcher paper, or perhaps to pick a name at random in order to award a prize.
- *Conduct a demonstration*. If the presentation involves a product demonstration, bring it to the meeting and have the audience use it. This approach can be deeply involving, but only if the product has been thoroughly tested in advance to ensure that even a neophyte user can get it right.
- *Conduct an exercise*. It can be useful to periodically conduct an exercise with the audience that is targeted at using the information that was just imparted.
- *Facilitate a discussion*. One of the best ways to involve the audience is for the speaker to take on the role of a facilitator, with most of the discussion actually occurring amongst the audience. The facilitator's role is to advance the discussion in the areas of his or her key points, and not let the conversation wander.
- *Give away a prize*. A great way to break up the presentation *and* involve the audience is to schedule a prize giveaway at regular intervals during the day.

A person's name is chosen at random and a minor gift awarded, such as a coffee mug or a relevant book.

- *Pose a question*. Ask the audience a question, and write down their responses on a flip chart. Their responses can then be integrated into the presentation. This approach can also be used at regular intervals to ensure that they understand the subject matter, using an open-ended question, such as "any issues with this so far" or "how would this work in your department?"
- *Tell a story*. Telling an involving story can grab the attention of the audience far more than a dry recitation of bullet points. The best ones are told from personal experience, since they are easy to recall and you are more emotionally linked to them – which shows. Just remember to keep them short.
- *Use humor*. An easy and effective involvement tool is to drop a humorous quote, joke, cartoon, or video clip into a presentation – just make sure that it is appropriate for the audience. Humor can break up an otherwise tedious talk, or reinforce a key point.

The most involving presentations will include a number of the preceding options, so that the audience is fully engaged with the subject matter.

The Difficult Audience Member

Sometimes, there is someone in the audience who appears to be out to get you. He poses difficult questions, monopolizes the conversation, complains about the presentation, and nitpicks your comments. What can be done? Here are several ideas:

- *Shut him down politely*. A person might issue a string of questions or a series of follow-up questions that take over the question and answer period. When this happens, just answer the first question, make a statement about giving other people a chance to ask questions, and move along to the next person. If the person continues to be disruptive, make a statement that you would be willing to meet with him afterwards to discuss the issue further.
- *Address the logic*. The person may be mean, but the question could actually be a good one. Try to separate the person's attitude from the question, and just answer the question. If you can keep your emotions out of your response, the audience will respect you for it.
- *Exercise empathy*. It is entirely possible that a pissed-off questioner has a right to be; if so, find out what is going on, and then answer their question from a more empathetic perspective. Such as, "Yes, I can totally see why you were upset about that customer service call."
- *Find common ground*. If there is *any* common ground between you and the questioner, acknowledge it. For example, "yes, I think we can both agree that customer service needs a lot of improvement."

Body Language

A presentation is conducted with the voice and the body. Even the finest voice presentation effort may bounce off an audience when your body language is telling them a different story. This can be corrected by paying attention to your body movement, eye communication, facial expressions, gestures, and posture. In the following sub-sections, we will go over the various improvements that can be made.

Better Body Movement

How you move around in front of the audience tells a story all by itself. Since your movement is a way of talking to the audience, use it by getting out from behind the lectern. This may involve, for example, walking up to (or amongst) the audience, leaning on the side of the lectern, or walking up to the screen to point out a feature on a slide.

> **Tip:** If the only available microphone is attached to a lectern, arrange to have a lapel microphone or something similar, to enable you to walk around.

Consider using body movement to signal a change to a new talking point. For example, as you shift from the first bullet point to the second one on a slide, move slightly to a new position on the stage, to indicate that you are switching to a new topic. Further, whenever you want to make a key point, step towards the audience as you make it, to drive home the point.

> **Tip:** Moving constantly around the stage implies that you are nervous or perhaps drank too much caffeine beforehand. Instead, only move as a point of emphasis, and stand still the rest of the time.

For example, a skilled presenter might walk up to the audience and deliver a short introductory speech, then access the first slide and walk over to the screen to expound upon a key point, then walk to the lectern to pick up an object that he wants to present to the audience, and then carry it into the audience to encourage them to touch it. Each of these movements is designed to support the presentation.

A final point is to work all sides of the room; do not favor one side and ignore the other. This means walking to one side, talking to the people over there for a short time, and then moving to the other side and giving them the same treatment (and don't forget the middle!). Doing so gives them the strong impression that you are equally approachable. However, your beginning comments and ending statements should be delivered from the center of the room, in order to give all participants equal access.

Effective Eye Communication

It is essential to maintain eye contact with the audience; doing so projects an air of sincerity and confidence. In addition, maintaining eye contact with the audience can settle your nerves, since the audience is usually supportive; you are more likely to pick up on this by looking in their eyes. Not looking at the audience creates an entirely different impression with them. They will think that you are refusing to look at them, which implies that you are shifty and insincere, and therefore not to be trusted.

Effective communication can be quite hard to do when you are struggling with the basics of the presentation. Consequently, you need a firm grounding in the subject matter before working on eye contact. If you can attain the requisite level of expertise, then the next step is to set a target of achieving meaningful eye contact with as many people in the audience as possible. In a small audience, this should be every person present.

It is certainly acceptable to look away from the audience occasionally, perhaps to look at your notes or to point out something on the screen. Other than these brief moments, however, your gaze should always be focused out on the audience. This does not mean a general sweep of the audience, but rather focusing on each individual person in turn, eye-to-eye. A good way to do this is to initially search for those people you have already met, perhaps while greeting people at the door. Talk directly to each one of them in turn for perhaps three seconds, just enough to establish a connection. Then move outward beyond these familiar faces to engage with everyone else in the room. Eventually (unless it is a *very* large audience), you should have looked at every person there.

Use your eyes to support the message. If the topic is serious (such as a layoff), then adopt a serious look with your eyes. If the topic is more cheerful (such as the annual employee bonus), then adopt a happier look. By doing so, your eye communication is aligned with your verbal message.

Another use of effective eye communication is to watch the nonverbal behavior of the audience. This can be quite useful to see if your message is getting across. For example, if they look confused, you might want to stop and ask if they understand what you are saying, and then adjust the presentation to deal with it. Once they register a look of understanding, it is time to continue with the presentation. Another possibility is that they cannot hear you. If so, ask if that is the case, and stop to adjust the microphone. Another possibility (especially if the topic is a technical one) is that the audience is in need of a break. This is evidenced by restlessness, yawning, heavy eyelids, and so forth. If so, possibilities are to insert some interaction with the audience, or wrap up the presentation, or call a short break.

Here are a few other best practices to consider to improve your level of eye communication with the audience:

- *Avoid eyeglasses*. Eyeglasses obscure your eyes and so make it more difficult to communicate with the audience. If you absolutely cannot do without them, then at least take them off from time to time in order to emphasize a point during the presentation.
- *Avoid scanning*. Do not scan back and forth across the audience. You are not looking them in the eye; instead, the audience will gain the strong impression that you are going through the motions by shifting your head in the correct manner, without actually looking at each of them individually.

- *Avoid the downward stare.* Those who are nervous or who are not sufficiently familiar with the materials will likely ignore the audience in favor of looking straight down at their notes. While this is more likely to ensure a technically accurate presentation, ignoring the audience will not exactly create a connection with the audience.
- *Equalize the attention.* The general goal is to give everyone in the room an equal amount of attention. There are a few exceptions, however. For example, if you are talking about a point that is a particular concern to one person in the room, then look at him or her while discussing it. Also, when completing the presentation and making final points, the bulk of your attention should be on the decision makers in the room.
- *Extend the look.* It is better to look directly at a person for a longer period of time than for a shorter period. Therefore, avoid the one-second glance in favor of the four or five-second glance.
- *Randomize the look.* Rather than scanning in a fixed pattern, look around the room and engage with people at random. This appears more natural to the audience.

Positive Facial Expressions

Anyone displaying a genuine smile is more likely to attract the audience, while someone grimacing will repel them. A smile conveys empathy and friendliness, and implies that you are interested in both the audience and the topic. Further, use your expressions to convey how you feel about any topic – evince wonder at the discussion of a miraculous African sunrise by raising your eyebrows, or look like you are pondering a deep point when recalling an old story from your childhood.

The audience will likely mirror your expressions, so when you see the audience looking tense, it is entirely possible that they are getting it from you. If so, you may be taking the presentation too seriously, which might be triggering a frown. If so, mentally reset your gestures and see if this has an impact on the facial expressions of the audience.

Supportive Gestures

Gestures can be used to visually support an idea or an emotion. That being the case, it makes sense to watch yourself in a mirror while practicing a presentation, to see if you can incorporate supportive gestures, such as holding a hand outward with the palm facing out to suggest resistance to a particular idea. Or, the classic arms thrown wide to indicate the size of the fish you caught. Another possibility when working through a list of bullet points is to count them off on your fingers as you go through them. As another example, if you want people to raise their hands if they have done something (such as buy a competitor's product within the last month) then raise your hand first.

> **Tip:** Using gestures frequently is also a great way to dissipate nervous energy, while at the same time appearing more accessible to the audience.

Here are a few other best practices to consider when trying to improve your use of gestures:

- *Some gesturing is always good.* Or, stated differently, no gesturing at all looks quite *un*natural, so try to punctuate what you are saying with some sort of accompanying gesture that looks natural. A reserved person will probably gesture less, while a more animated person might appear to be more caffeinated, but in both cases, some amount of gesturing is expected.
- *Go big.* Gesturing should be expansive, which means starting at the shoulders, not the elbows. Otherwise, it looks like your upper arms are glued to your sides. Most gesturing is at the waist level, though an occasional motion up over the head is indicative of a major point.
- *Rest at the sides.* When not being used for gesturing, your arms should be at your sides. Though this may seem awkward to you, it appears relaxed to the audience. This should be your default position when not gesturing. However, this only appears relaxed if you are not fidgeting at the same time.
- *No crossed arms.* Crossing your arms might appear to be a good way to do something with your arms, but it also signals that you are closing yourself off from the audience. However, it can be useful occasionally as a signal that you are pondering, perhaps in response to a question from the audience.
- *No clasping.* Do not clasp your hands, either in front of you or behind.
- *Go full immersion.* If you are fully immersed in your topic, then your gestures will flow automatically, and you will not have to worry about any of the preceding points.

Enhanced Posture

The general guideline for proper posture is to stand fully upright (no slouching) and well-balanced. Doing so improves your breathing and therefore your voice, and also projects a higher degree of confidence to the audience. A few pointers on how to achieve better posture are to pull in your stomach, keep your chin up, pull back your shoulders, and keep most of your weight forward on the balls of your feet. However, do not go so far with the concept that you are exhibiting a military "at attention" bearing.

Your Speaking Voice

There are several ways to enhance your speaking voice. It is very much to your advantage to do so, since it can greatly increase the persuasiveness of your presentation. Here are several possible avenues to pursue:

- *Pronunciation enhancement.* This involves speaking a word correctly, based on its phonetic spelling. For example, "would you" is properly pronounced as "wood yoo" and not "woodja". Or, "nuclear" is properly pronounced as "noo klee ar" and not "nook u lar".

- *Articulation enhancement*. This is the ability to speak clearly and distinctly, so that each word is pronounced correctly and enunciated properly. Conversely, examples of inadequate articulation are mumbling and trailing off at the end of a sentence. Proper articulation makes it much easier to understand the speaker. Articulation can be improved by practicing a speech at slow speed, deliberately forming each word.
- *Pace enhancement*. This is the rate at which you speak. The ideal pacing is about 150 words per minute, which balances between a slow drone and the embarrassing chipmunk speed of a nervous speaker. This pace can be somewhat faster when breezing through a story, and slower when talking about a detailed analysis. Your pace can be easily checked by reading from a written speech for one minute, and then counting the words completed. Recording your latest speech and listening to the recording will give you a good idea of whether your pacing is reasonable. An additional possibility is to include the words "slow down" as a reminder at various points in the presentation.
- *Pitch enhancement*. This is how high or low you speak. Ideally, the bulk of your message should be spoken in the mid-range, with high and low points reserved to emphasize specific points in the presentation. Generally, a voice pitched low is considered to be more authoritative and credible.
- *Tone enhancement*. Your tone of voice is how you say something. You can adjust it to convey how you feel about what is being said. Tone should strongly support what it is that you are saying. It can convey such emotions as urgency, sincerity, or friendliness. When practicing a speech, try to include your desired tone in the practice sessions. Recording and then reviewing a practice session for tone is a good way to improve.
- *Inflection enhancement*. This is the use of modulation in your pace, pitch, or tone in order to place emphasis on particular statements within a presentation. The reverse is speaking in a monotone, which is sure to put the audience in a catatonic state. A good way to include inflection points in a presentation is to point them out in the presentation notes, using bold, italics, underlining and so forth. In particular, inflect downward at the end of a sentence in order to avoid making every sentence sound like a question. A downward inflection makes you sound much more confident about what you are saying.
- *Volume enhancement*. Good voice projection is an essential part of public speaking. To improve it, use deep, controlled breathing. Also, talk straight out at the audience, rather than down at the lectern or back at the projection screen.
- *Filler elimination*. It is all too common for a speaker to fill in blank spots in a speech with fillers, such as "ummm" or "you know," typically while the speaker is searching for the next substantive point to make. This is most common when the speaker is unprepared, so the obvious solution is to prepare early and often for each speech. Recording a speech and playing it back is a good way to determine whether this is a significant problem.

Effective Phrasing

A speech should contain words that are specifically targeted at persuading the audience. The phrasing used by the speaker should drive straight to the heart of the matter under discussion, and then propose a course of action in the simplest terms. How does a persuasive speaker do this? Here are several ways in which they arrive at effective phrasing:

- *Focus on them.* The speech focuses on "you" rather than "me," so that the speaker emphasizes that the presentation is all about the audience. Consider recording a presentation and reviewing it to see if your emphasis is really on the audience. Also, the more questions you ask of the audience, the more they will come to believe that you are prioritizing their best interests.
- *Use action verbs.* The repeated use of action verbs results in a more invigorating presentation, on which the audience is more likely to take action. Therefore, all bullet points on a slide should begin with an action verb, such as control, eliminate, generate, manage, manufacture, save, and use. There are hundreds of additional possibilities (conduct a Google search on "list of action verbs" for more possibilities).
- *State logical outcomes.* Use phrasing that shows a logical outcome if the audience takes action. For example, "You've heard how 15 customers have been able to dig power line ditches at twice the normal speed. Therefore, we can assist you in achieving your goal of completing the fiber optic cable installation by the end of this year."
- *Sell the benefits.* Make it quite clear what the benefits will be for the audience; don't rely on them to figure it out. For example, "This swimming pool automatically rolls out a pool cover when no one is nearby. The bottom line for you is less evaporation, so your water bills will go down."
- *Incorporate power words.* Some words help users to visualize how they will feel if they take your advice. Using these words repeatedly will make customers more likely to take action. Examples of these words are "you'll save time," "reduce the hassle," and "you'll save money."
- *Eliminate weak words.* Opposing power words are other words that are much too passive to put into a presentation. Since they cannot be used to project force, they are unlikely to spark a response from the audience. Examples are, "*hopefully*, we can get this deal done," "*if* this is acceptable to you, we can finalize the paperwork," and "I was *wondering* if your criteria vary much from this list?" In short, never use these words.
- *Avoid hedging statements.* Any sort of hedging statement signals that you are not fully behind your presentation; when that is the impression, the audience may well ask itself why it should follow your recommendations. An example of a hedging statement is, "it appears more likely than not that our new toothpaste reduces tooth decay."

The Dress Code

While it is important not to dress much more or less formally than the audience, it is critical to arrive at a dress code that improves the audience's impression of you. Here are a few pointers:

- *Colors*. Stick with conservative suit colors, such as navy or dark gray. Anything brighter distracts from the presentation.
- *Patterns*. Solid or light pinstripes are good; most other patterns are too distracting, and so should be avoided.
- *Fabric*. A wool, silk, or blended fabric conveys a higher-quality image than anything synthetic. Shirts and blouses should be 100% cotton or silk.
- *Tailoring*. Go for a well-tailored look; not too tight or too baggy.
- *Pressing*. Clothing should be professionally cleaned, to eliminate any hint of a home pressing or inadequate cleaning activities.
- *Sleeves*. Full-length sleeves are considered standard for business presentations.
- *Shoes*. Your shoes should be adequately polished and therefore free of scuffs.
- *Jewelry*. Whatever jewelry worn should be at a minimal level; it should not distract the audience.
- *Glasses*. If you must wear glasses, only use ones with an anti-reflective coating, so that the audience can more easily see your eyes. Do not use tinted lenses, for the same reason.

The Importance of a Quality Presentation

The amount of work that goes into a presentation can have a startling impact on the outcome. Consider, for example, a presentation for the sale of accounting software to a company. Eight firms have been invited to make presentations to the CFO, controller, and accounting employees of the company. What really differentiates these eight firms from each other? After all, most accounting software packages have the same features and are capable of processing transactions in the same way. The firm that won probably went through the steps just described for developing a persuasive presentation, learning as much detail about the audience as possible, as well as its needs, and then crafting a presentation that focused tightly on those needs. In short, even though any of the eight firms could have won the competition, the firm that actually did so put more effort into its presentation.

The same situation arises when making presentations to others within the company. The person who puts the most effort into his or her presentations is the one who comes across as more polished and professional, and so will be more likely to be given the choicest assignments and eventually promoted. In short, a quality presentation can be the defining factor for people and companies, and so can result in major differences in profitability (for companies) and career advancement (for employees).

Foreign Language Presentations

It is increasingly common to be asked to make a presentation in another country. If so, you may need to work with an interpreter during the presentation. This may involve a simultaneous translation, where the interpreter sits in a soundproof booth and the translated version is transmitted to earphones worn by the audience. This approach has relatively minimal impact on the speaker, who can proceed at a normal pace. However, in a more budget-conscious environment, the speaker and translator trade off, with the speaker talking for a few sentences and then pausing long enough for the translator to say the same thing in the local language. In the latter case, the interaction between the speaker and translator is critical, so if there is any tension between the two, it will be readily apparent to the audience. To keep this from happening, and if there is a choice of translators, interview them to see which one you are most comfortable with.

A few additional points relating to foreign language translations are:

- *Content length.* When the translator is going to be trading off with you, cut the content length to half of what you normally present. This is needed to account for the extra time required by the translator.
- *Send notes.* Send the most recent version of the presentation notes to the translator a few days in advance, so that he or she can engage in some advance preparation.
- *Practice.* Schedule a practice session with the translator, mostly to gain an understanding of the amount of material that she is capable of translating at a time. In addition, find out the talking speed at which she is most comfortable; it is likely that you will need to slow down somewhat, so that she can keep up. These changes may require you to speak in a shorter and choppier style, in order to state complete thoughts with fewer words; doing so makes it easier for the translator to translate these statements for the audience.

For Those Who Have Difficulty Presenting

Many of us have difficulty making presentations, for any number of reasons. We may be uncomfortable standing in front of a group, or we are overawed by the more powerful people in the audience, or perhaps we are none too certain about the contents of the presentation. Or maybe we just don't want to have our performance evaluated, or don't know how the message will be received. These are mostly illusions that will not actually happen, but they can have a powerful impact on how you feel. There are several ways to get around these issues. Consider the following:

- *Visualize it.* See yourself delivering a successful presentation, speaking confidently to an attentive audience. This can be a self-fulfilling prophecy. At worst, a positive visualization of what might happen will crowd out any negative visualizations, which still leaves you ahead of the game.

- *Practice.* Always practice a presentation in advance, preferably several times. Doing so allows you to iron out any bugs in the presentation, and improves your comfort level with the presentation materials. It can also help to present in front of a friendly audience, such as your spouse, who can provide advice on how to improve the presentation. Further, do a full dress rehearsal, wearing the same clothes you expect to wear during the presentation, and in a similar environment. Doing so accustoms you to exactly what will happen on stage.

Note: If you have not rehearsed a presentation in advance, then the actual presentation will *be* the rehearsal – and the audience will see it.

- *Memorize the front end.* The hardest part is starting a presentation, so spend triple the amount of practice time on just the first few sentences. This minimizes the risk of freezing up at the start. Once you get going, the nerves tend to recede, making the rest of the presentation that much easier.
- *Record it.* It can be useful to record your presentation, and listen to how you are presenting. A common takeaway is that you are speaking too fast, so use this feedback loop to control your speaking speed.

Tip: Listen to the recording of your presentation while driving to work. In this relaxed environment, you can work on memorizing key sections of the speech, and note which items need to be changed.

- *Exercise.* The mind tends to dwell on the bad things that might happen if the body is sedentary. So don't be – go for a walk, and set a good pace. The exercise is good for you, and it can push away the demons. At a minimum, perform a few stretches backstage.
- *Listen to music.* Athletes are always listening to music just before their events. There is a reason for this, as it calms them down. The same approach works with presentations. Prepare a playlist of your favorite musicians, and play it shortly before each presentation.
- *Breathe deep.* Other than being part of the lyrics to a great Moody Blues tune, breathing slowly and deeply is a great way to settle yourself down. It also concentrates the mind, since you are focusing on the breathing pattern.
- *Greet them.* Stand outside the meeting room and greet everyone as they arrive. By doing so, you have made eye contact and communicated (however briefly) with the attendees, which may lower your sense of nervousness.
- *Tell them.* If you are nervous, say so. Ask the audience for their patience and assistance, which may trigger some degree of empathy for your situation; after all, many of the people in the audience may also be nervous when they are asked to make presentations.
- *Involve them.* Get the audience involved in some way within the first few minutes, perhaps with a question or a quick survey. By doing so, the focus shifts from you to the audience, thereby reducing the pressure on you. Also,

it lets you know that there are people out there who want to participate in what you are doing.

- *Anticipate tough questions.* Dream up the most difficult questions that someone could possibly ask, and craft good responses to them. If you are prepared for the hard questions, you should be able to rest easy in regard to all other questions.

How Not to Present

Thus far, we have only talked about techniques for creating a great, persuasive presentation. However, it can also be useful to be aware of the ways in which a presentation can be ruined, in order to avoid them. A less-successful presentation probably involves one or more of the following:

- *Too much information.* The presenter dumps far too much information on the audience. Doing so is not only confusing, it also wastes the time of the audience. A solid indicator of too much information is when the audience becomes restive and interrupts the speaker.
- *Disorganized.* The presenter has not developed a coherent presentation, so the talk rambles from one unrelated point to the next, eventually petering out with no clear conclusion. When this happens, expect someone in the audience to ask for clarity regarding the point of the presentation, or to simply walk out.
- *Needs disconnect.* The presenter has not tied the main message of the presentation to the needs of the audience, likely due to a lack of research regarding their needs. A likely outcome is a zero win rate with the audience – no sales or converts have been made.
- *Timid.* The presenter is not committed to the material; instead, he is just reading from the slides or notes, rarely looks at the audience, and has no apparent interest in ensuring that the audience adopts his message. Expect no converts when the presenter is timid.
- *Minimal support.* The presenter has not assembled any solid, supporting detail that backs up his case. Instead, the presentation only contains a few statements of fact, which are hardly likely to convince the audience.
- *Fumbles questions.* The presenter has not anticipated any of the questions that are asked, and so has a difficult time responding to any objections that are raised. The audience is likely to leave the room unconvinced.
- *Pushes back.* The presenter is defensive when asked probing questions. The point of these questions is to clarify points made during the presentation and so are not intended to be personal attacks – and yet the presenter takes them personally. This is a strong sign of immaturity, so the audience cannot be expected to ask the presenter back for a repeat performance.

The preparatory steps noted earlier in this book are intended to keep all of the preceding presentation problems from happening. If it appears that you have fallen into one of these traps, go back and review the source materials. It is likely that additional preparation will keep them from happening again.

Summary

The key to a persuasive presentation is in preparation, preparation, and more preparation. It involves researching the audience, developing the message to present to them, identifying the best possible media to use, developing slides, practicing the presentation, conducting the actual presentation, taking questions, and measuring the outcome. But that is not all – you also need to work on building a connection with the audience, which involves improving your body language, speaking voice, and phrasing, as well as dressing appropriately for the part. These tasks are hardly easy, so do not expect to accomplish them all at once and suddenly become an outstanding presenter. Instead, expect to work on these activities, in detail, over an extended period of time, before mastering them. For those whose livelihoods are closely tied to their presentation skills, this is a worthy art to pursue.

To gather more information about high-quality presentations, go to slideshare.net and ted.com to view professional presentations made by other parties, as well as the unique features of the slides they used.

Glossary

A

Articulation. The ability to speak clearly and distinctly, so that each word is pronounced correctly and enunciated properly.

F

Forgetting curve. A hypothesis that the amount of information retained in memory declines over time.

I

Inflection. The use of modulation in one's pace, pitch or tone in order to place emphasis on particular statements within a presentation.

P

Pace. The rate at which a person speaks.

Persuasion. The process of changing a person's attitude or behavior toward something.

Pitch. How high or low a person speaks.

Pronunciation. Speaking a word correctly, based on its phonetic spelling.

T

Tone. How a person says something, to convey how he or she feels about what is being said.

Index

www.ingramcontent.com/pod-product-compliance
Lightning Source LLC
Chambersburg PA
CBHW080722220326
41520CB00056B/7371